Motherhood

ISBN: 1-933662-06-9

This book may be ordered by mail from the publisher. Please include $3.50 for postage and handling. Please support your local bookseller first!

Books published by Cider mill Press Book Publishers are available at special discounts for bulk purchases in the United States by corporations, institutions, and other organizations. For more information, please contact the publisher.

Cider Mill Press Book Publishers
"Where good books are ready for press"
12 Port Farm Road
Kennebunkport, Maine 04046

Visit us on the web!
www.cidermillpress.com

Cover Photograph by: John Whalen
Photography Subject: The author with her first-born child
Cover Design by: Lana Mullen
Design by: Julie Reynolds and David Page
Typography: Edwardian Script ITC

Special thanks to David Page, who has never lost his spirit from childhood.

Printed in China
1 2 3 4 5 6 7 8 9 0
First Edition

Motherhood

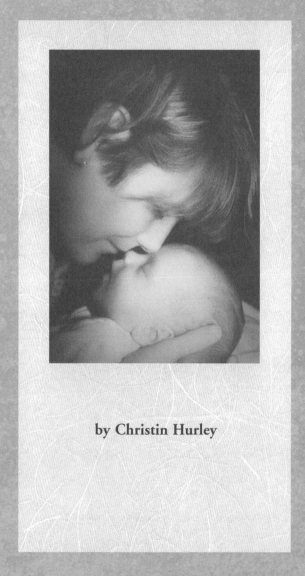

by Christin Hurley

A Guided Journal with Inspiring Quotes

CIDER MILL PRESS

For my three sons... without them I would not be whole.

Christin Hurley

Being a full-time mother is one of the highest salaried jobs… since the payment is pure love.

Mildred B. Vermont

A mother holds her children's hands for a while, their hearts forever.

Author Unknown

Mother love is the fuel that enables a normal human being to do the impossible.
Marion C. Garretty

What is home without a mother?

Alice Hawthorne

_____

_____

_____

_____

_____

_____

_____

_____

_____

_____

_____

_____

_____

_____

_____

_____

_____

_____

_____

_____

_____

_____

_____

_____

_____

_____

_____

Mother's arms are made of tenderness, and sweet sleep blesses the child who lies therein.

Victor Hugo

The heart of a mother is a deep abyss at the bottom of which you will always find forgiveness.

Honoré de Balzac

The mother's heart is the child's schoolroom.

Henry Ward Beecher

A mother is the truest friend we have, when trials, heavy and sudden, fall upon us; when adversity takes the place of prosperity; when friends who rejoice with us in our sunshine, desert us when troubles thicken around us, still will she cling to us, and endeavor by her kind precepts and counsels to dissipate the clouds of darkness, and cause peace to return to our hearts.

Washington Irving

Youth fades, love droops, the leaves of friendship fall;
A mother's secret hope outlives them all.

Oliver Wendell Holmes

To understand a mother's love, bear your own children.

Chinese Proverb

*Mother is the name for God on the lips
and in the hearts of little children.*

William Makepeace Thackeray

Who is it that loves me and will love me forever with an affection which no chance, no misery, no crime of mine can do away?--It is you, my mother.

Thomas Carlyle

When God thought of mother, He must have laughed with satisfaction, and framed it quickly- -so rich, so deep, so divine, so full of soul, power, and beauty, was the conception.

Henry Ward Beecher

I think my life began with waking up and loving my mother's face.

George Eliot

Mothers reflect God's

loving presence on earth.

William R. Webb

There is no friendship, no love, like that of the parent for the child.
Henry Ward Beecher

A mother is a person who seeing there are only four pieces of pie for five people, promptly announces she never did care for pie.

Tenneva Jordan

Only mothers can think of the future--because they give birth to it in their children.

Maxim Gorky

The moment a child is born, the mother is also born. She never existed before. The woman existed, but the mother, never. A mother is something absolutely new.

Bhagwan Rajneesh

The sweetest sounds to mortals given
Are heard in Mother, Home, and Heaven.

William Goldsmith Brown

[A] mother is one to whom you hurry when you are troubled.

Emily Dickinson

Before you were conceived
I wanted you.
Before you were born I loved you.
Before you were here an hour
I would die for you.
This is the miracle of life.

Maureen Hawkins

Mother's love is peace. It need not be acquired, it need not be deserved.
Erich Fromm

A little girl, asked where her home was, replied 'where mother is.'
Keith L. Brooks

Most of all the other beautiful things in life come by twos and threes, by dozens and hundreds. Plenty of roses, stars, sunsets, rainbows, brothers and sisters, aunts and cousins, comrades and friends--but only one mother in the whole world.

Kate Douglas Wiggin

There never was a woman like her. She was gentle as a dove and brave as a lioness . . . The memory of my mother and her teachings were, after all, the only capital I had to start life with, and on that capital I have made my way.

Andrew Jackson

I look back on my childhood and thank the stars above.
For everything you gave me, but mostly for your love.

Wayne F. Winters

A mother is someone who dreams great dreams for you, but then she lets you chase the dreams you have for yourself and loves you just the same.

Author Unknown

It seems to me that my mother was the most splendid woman I ever knew...I have met a lot of people knocking around the world since, but I have never met a more thoroughly refined woman than my mother. If I have amounted to anything, it will be due to her.

Charles Chaplin

All that I am my mother made me.

John Quincy Adams

_____
_____
_____
_____
_____
_____
_____
_____
_____
_____
_____
_____
_____
_____
_____
_____
_____
_____
_____
_____
_____
_____
_____
_____
_____
_____
_____
_____

A mother's children are portraits of herself.

Author Unknown

A mother is she who can take the place of all others but whose place no one else can take.

Cardinal Mermillod

_____

_____

_____

_____

_____

_____

_____

_____

_____

_____

_____

_____

_____

_____

_____

_____

_____

_____

_____

_____

_____

_____

_____

_____

_____

Mothers are the pivot on which the family spins.
Mothers are the pivot on which the world spins.

Pam Brown

_____
_____
_____
_____
_____
_____
_____
_____
_____
_____
_____
_____
_____
_____
_____
_____
_____
_____
_____
_____
_____
_____
_____
_____
_____
_____
_____

A mother is not a person to lean on, but a person to make leaning unnecessary.
Dorothy Canfield Fisher

Mother is the heartbeat in the home; and without her, there seems to be no heart throb.

Leroy Brownlow

_____

_____

_____

_____

_____

_____

_____

_____

_____

_____

_____

_____

_____

_____

_____

_____

_____

_____

_____

_____

_____

_____

_____

_____

_____

_____

_____

Raising kids is part joy

and part guerilla warfare.

Ed Asner

A child is a curly, dimpled lunatic.

Ralph Waldo Emerson

Invest in the future: have a child and teach her well.

Author Unknown

I have found the best way to give advice to your children is to find out what they want and then advise them to do it.

Harry S. Truman

Every mother is like Moses. She does not enter the promised land. She prepares a world she will not see.

Pope Paul VI

_____
_____
_____
_____
_____
_____
_____
_____
_____
_____
_____
_____
_____
_____
_____
_____
_____
_____
_____
_____
_____
_____
_____
_____
_____
_____
_____
_____

Mothers are the most instinctive philosophers.

Harriet Beecher Stowe

Of all the rights of women, the greatest is to be a mother.

Lin Yutang

*God could not be everywhere
and therefore he made mothers.*

Jewish Proverb